MW01035142

JIU-JITSU

TRAINING JOURNAL

Copyright © 2019 by Combat Arts Press
All rights reserved. No part of this publication may be reproduced, distributed, or
transmitted in any form or by any means, including photocopying, recording, or other
electronic or mechanical methods, without the prior written permission of the publisher.

DATES	CONTENT

POSITION: _____ TECHNIQUE: _____

KEY DETAILS: _____

_____

_____

_____

_____

_____

_____

POSITION: _____ TECHNIQUE: _____

KEY DETAILS: _____

_____

_____

_____

_____

_____

TRAINING PARTNER: NOTES: GOAL: _____

_____

_____

_____

_____

_____

ONE IMPORTANT THING I WANT TO REMEMBER ABOUT TODAY:

_____

_____

_____

DATE: _____ INSTRUCTOR: _____

BELT RANK: _____ WEIGHT: _____ ☐ GI ☐ NOGI ☐ BOTH

POSITION: _____ TECHNIQUE: _____

KEY DETAILS: _____

_____

_____

_____

_____

_____

_____

POSITION: _____ TECHNIQUE: _____

KEY DETAILS: _____

_____

_____

_____

_____

_____

_____

POSITION: _____ TECHNIQUE: _____

KEY DETAILS: _____

_____

_____

_____

_____

_____

_____

POSITION: _____ **TECHNIQUE:** _____

KEY DETAILS: _____

_____

_____

_____

_____

_____

_____

_____

POSITION: _____ **TECHNIQUE:** _____

KEY DETAILS: _____

_____

_____

_____

_____

_____

_____

TRAINING PARTNER: **NOTES:**   **GOAL:** _____

_____

_____

_____

_____

_____

_____

ONE IMPORTANT THING I WANT TO REMEMBER ABOUT TODAY:

_____

_____

_____

DATE: .... INSTRUCTOR: ....

BELT RANK: .... WEIGHT: .... ☐ GI ☐ NOGI ☐ BOTH

POSITION: .... TECHNIQUE: ....

KEY DETAILS: ....

....

....

....

....

....

....

....

POSITION: .... TECHNIQUE: ....

KEY DETAILS: ....

....

....

....

....

....

....

....

POSITION: .... TECHNIQUE: ....

KEY DETAILS: ....

....

....

....

....

....

....

....

POSITION: .... TECHNIQUE: ....

KEY DETAILS: ....

_____

_____

_____

_____

_____

_____

_____

_____

POSITION: .... TECHNIQUE: ....

KEY DETAILS: ....

_____

_____

_____

_____

_____

_____

TRAINING PARTNER: NOTES: GOAL: ....

ONE IMPORTANT THING I WANT TO REMEMBER ABOUT TODAY:

DATE: .... INSTRUCTOR: ....

BELT RANK: .... WEIGHT: .... ☐ GI ☐ NOGI ☐ BOTH

POSITION: .... TECHNIQUE: ....

KEY DETAILS: ....

....

....

....

....

....

....

POSITION: .... TECHNIQUE: ....

KEY DETAILS: ....

....

....

....

....

....

....

POSITION: .... TECHNIQUE: ....

KEY DETAILS: ....

....

....

....

....

....

....

POSITION: .... TECHNIQUE: ....
KEY DETAILS: ....

....

....

....

....

....

....

POSITION: .... TECHNIQUE: ....
KEY DETAILS: ....

....

....

....

....

TRAINING PARTNER: NOTES: GOAL: ....

....

....

....

....

....

ONE IMPORTANT THING I WANT TO REMEMBER ABOUT TODAY:

....

....

DATE: _____ INSTRUCTOR: _____

BELT RANK: _____ WEIGHT: _____ ☐ GI ☐ NOGI ☐ BOTH

POSITION: _____ TECHNIQUE: _____

KEY DETAILS: _____

_____

_____

_____

_____

_____

_____

_____

POSITION: _____ TECHNIQUE: _____

KEY DETAILS: _____

_____

_____

_____

_____

_____

_____

_____

POSITION: _____ TECHNIQUE: _____

KEY DETAILS: _____

_____

_____

_____

_____

_____

_____

_____

POSITION: _____ TECHNIQUE: _____

KEY DETAILS: _____

_____

_____

_____

_____

_____

_____

_____

POSITION: _____ TECHNIQUE: _____

KEY DETAILS: _____

_____

_____

_____

_____

_____

_____

_____

TRAINING PARTNER:	NOTES:	GOAL:

ONE IMPORTANT THING I WANT TO REMEMBER ABOUT TODAY:

_____

_____

_____

DATE: .... INSTRUCTOR: ....

BELT RANK: .... WEIGHT: .... ☐ GI ☐ NOGI ☐ BOTH

POSITION: .... TECHNIQUE: ....
KEY DETAILS: ....

_____

_____

_____

_____

_____

_____

POSITION: .... TECHNIQUE: ....
KEY DETAILS: ....

_____

_____

_____

_____

_____

_____

POSITION: .... TECHNIQUE: ....
KEY DETAILS: ....

_____

_____

_____

_____

_____

_____

POSITION: _____ TECHNIQUE: _____

KEY DETAILS: _____

_____

_____

_____

_____

_____

_____

_____

POSITION: _____ TECHNIQUE: _____

KEY DETAILS: _____

_____

_____

_____

_____

_____

_____

TRAINING PARTNER: NOTES: GOAL: _____

_____   _____

_____   _____

_____   _____

_____   _____

_____   _____

ONE IMPORTANT THING I WANT TO REMEMBER ABOUT TODAY:

_____

_____

_____

DATE: .... INSTRUCTOR: ....

BELT RANK: .... WEIGHT: .... ☐ GI ☐ NOGI ☐ BOTH

POSITION: .... TECHNIQUE: ....
KEY DETAILS: ....

_____

_____

_____

_____

_____

_____

_____

POSITION: .... TECHNIQUE: ....
KEY DETAILS: ....

_____

_____

_____

_____

_____

_____

_____

POSITION: .... TECHNIQUE: ....
KEY DETAILS: ....

_____

_____

_____

_____

_____

_____

POSITION: _____ TECHNIQUE: _____

KEY DETAILS: _____

_____

_____

_____

_____

_____

_____

_____

POSITION: _____ TECHNIQUE: _____

KEY DETAILS: _____

_____

_____

_____

_____

_____

_____

TRAINING PARTNER: NOTES: GOAL: _____

_____ _____

_____ _____

_____ _____

_____ _____

_____ _____

ONE IMPORTANT THING I WANT TO REMEMBER ABOUT TODAY:

_____

_____

_____

DATE: .... INSTRUCTOR: ....

BELT RANK: .... WEIGHT: .... ☐ GI ☐ NOGI ☐ BOTH

POSITION: .... TECHNIQUE: ....

KEY DETAILS: ....

_____

_____

_____

_____

_____

_____

_____

POSITION: .... TECHNIQUE: ....

KEY DETAILS: ....

_____

_____

_____

_____

_____

_____

_____

POSITION: .... TECHNIQUE: ....

KEY DETAILS: ....

_____

_____

_____

_____

_____

_____

_____

POSITION: .... TECHNIQUE: ....
KEY DETAILS: ....

_____

_____

_____

_____

_____

_____

POSITION: .... TECHNIQUE: ....
KEY DETAILS: ....

_____

_____

_____

_____

_____

_____

TRAINING PARTNER: NOTES: GOAL: ....

ONE IMPORTANT THING I WANT TO REMEMBER ABOUT TODAY:

DATE: _____ INSTRUCTOR: _____

BELT RANK: _____ WEIGHT: _____ ☐ GI ☐ NOGI ☐ BOTH

POSITION: _____ TECHNIQUE: _____

KEY DETAILS: _____

_____

_____

_____

_____

_____

_____

POSITION: _____ TECHNIQUE: _____

KEY DETAILS: _____

_____

_____

_____

_____

_____

_____

POSITION: _____ TECHNIQUE: _____

KEY DETAILS: _____

_____

_____

_____

_____

_____

_____

POSITION: .... TECHNIQUE: ....
KEY DETAILS: ....

_____

_____

_____

_____

_____

_____

_____

POSITION: .... TECHNIQUE: ....
KEY DETAILS: ....

_____

_____

_____

_____

_____

_____

TRAINING PARTNER:	NOTES:	GOAL:

ONE IMPORTANT THING I WANT TO REMEMBER ABOUT TODAY:

_____

_____

_____

DATE: _____ INSTRUCTOR: _____

BELT RANK: _____ WEIGHT: _____ ☐ GI ☐ NOGI ☐ BOTH

POSITION: _____ TECHNIQUE: _____

KEY DETAILS: _____

_____

_____

_____

_____

_____

_____

_____

POSITION: _____ TECHNIQUE: _____

KEY DETAILS: _____

_____

_____

_____

_____

_____

_____

_____

POSITION: _____ TECHNIQUE: _____

KEY DETAILS: _____

_____

_____

_____

_____

_____

_____

POSITION: _____ TECHNIQUE: _____

KEY DETAILS: _____

_____

_____

_____

_____

_____

_____

_____

POSITION: _____ TECHNIQUE: _____

KEY DETAILS: _____

_____

_____

_____

_____

_____

TRAINING PARTNER:	NOTES:	GOAL: _____
_____		_____
_____		_____
_____		_____
_____		_____
_____		_____

ONE IMPORTANT THING I WANT TO REMEMBER ABOUT TODAY:

_____

_____

_____

DATE: _____ INSTRUCTOR: _____

BELT RANK: _____ WEIGHT: _____ ☐ GI ☐ NOGI ☐ BOTH

POSITION: _____ TECHNIQUE: _____

KEY DETAILS: _____

_____

_____

_____

_____

_____

_____

_____

POSITION: _____ TECHNIQUE: _____

KEY DETAILS: _____

_____

_____

_____

_____

_____

_____

_____

POSITION: _____ TECHNIQUE: _____

KEY DETAILS: _____

_____

_____

_____

_____

_____

_____

_____

POSITION: _____ TECHNIQUE: _____

KEY DETAILS: _____

_____

_____

_____

_____

_____

_____

_____

POSITION: _____ TECHNIQUE: _____

KEY DETAILS: _____

_____

_____

_____

_____

_____

_____

TRAINING PARTNER: NOTES: GOAL: _____

_____   _____

_____   _____

_____   _____

_____   _____

_____   _____

ONE IMPORTANT THING I WANT TO REMEMBER ABOUT TODAY:

_____

_____

_____

DATE: _____ INSTRUCTOR: _____

BELT RANK: _____ WEIGHT: _____ ☐ GI ☐ NOGI ☐ BOTH

POSITION: _____ TECHNIQUE: _____

KEY DETAILS: _____

_____

_____

_____

_____

_____

_____

POSITION: _____ TECHNIQUE: _____

KEY DETAILS: _____

_____

_____

_____

_____

_____

_____

POSITION: _____ TECHNIQUE: _____

KEY DETAILS: _____

_____

_____

_____

_____

_____

_____

POSITION: .... TECHNIQUE: ....

KEY DETAILS: ....

_____

_____

_____

_____

_____

_____

_____

POSITION: .... TECHNIQUE: ....

KEY DETAILS: ....

_____

_____

_____

_____

_____

TRAINING PARTNER: NOTES: GOAL: ....

ONE IMPORTANT THING I WANT TO REMEMBER ABOUT TODAY:

_____

_____

_____

DATE: .... INSTRUCTOR: ....

BELT RANK: .... WEIGHT: .... ☐ GI ☐ NOGI ☐ BOTH

POSITION: .... TECHNIQUE: ....

KEY DETAILS: ....

_____

_____

_____

_____

_____

_____

POSITION: .... TECHNIQUE: ....

KEY DETAILS: ....

_____

_____

_____

_____

_____

_____

POSITION: .... TECHNIQUE: ....

KEY DETAILS: ....

_____

_____

_____

_____

_____

_____

POSITION: _____ TECHNIQUE: _____

KEY DETAILS: _____

_____

_____

_____

_____

_____

_____

POSITION: _____ TECHNIQUE: _____

KEY DETAILS: _____

_____

_____

_____

_____

_____

_____

TRAINING PARTNER: NOTES: GOAL: _____

ONE IMPORTANT THING I WANT TO REMEMBER ABOUT TODAY:

_____

_____

_____

DATE: _____ INSTRUCTOR: _____

BELT RANK: _____ WEIGHT: _____ ☐ GI ☐ NOGI ☐ BOTH

POSITION: _____ TECHNIQUE: _____

KEY DETAILS: _____

_____

_____

_____

_____

_____

_____

POSITION: _____ TECHNIQUE: _____

KEY DETAILS: _____

_____

_____

_____

_____

_____

_____

POSITION: _____ TECHNIQUE: _____

KEY DETAILS: _____

_____

_____

_____

_____

_____

_____

POSITION: _____ TECHNIQUE: _____

KEY DETAILS: _____

_____

_____

_____

_____

_____

_____

_____

_____

POSITION: _____ TECHNIQUE: _____

KEY DETAILS: _____

_____

_____

_____

_____

_____

_____

_____

TRAINING PARTNER:	NOTES:	GOAL: _____
_____		_____
_____		_____
_____		_____
_____		_____
_____		_____

ONE IMPORTANT THING I WANT TO REMEMBER ABOUT TODAY:

_____

_____

_____

DATE: _____ INSTRUCTOR: _____

BELT RANK: _____ WEIGHT: _____ ☐ GI ☐ NOGI ☐ BOTH

POSITION: _____ TECHNIQUE: _____

KEY DETAILS: _____

_____

_____

_____

_____

_____

_____

_____

POSITION: _____ TECHNIQUE: _____

KEY DETAILS: _____

_____

_____

_____

_____

_____

_____

_____

POSITION: _____ TECHNIQUE: _____

KEY DETAILS: _____

_____

_____

_____

_____

_____

_____

POSITION: _____ TECHNIQUE: _____

KEY DETAILS: _____

_____

_____

_____

_____

_____

_____

_____

POSITION: _____ TECHNIQUE: _____

KEY DETAILS: _____

_____

_____

_____

_____

_____

TRAINING PARTNER:	NOTES:	GOAL:

ONE IMPORTANT THING I WANT TO REMEMBER ABOUT TODAY:

_____

_____

_____

DATE: .... INSTRUCTOR: ....

BELT RANK: .... WEIGHT: .... ☐ GI ☐ NOGI ☐ BOTH

POSITION: .... TECHNIQUE: ....

KEY DETAILS: ....

....

....

....

....

....

....

POSITION: .... TECHNIQUE: ....

KEY DETAILS: ....

....

....

....

....

....

....

POSITION: .... TECHNIQUE: ....

KEY DETAILS: ....

....

....

....

....

....

....

POSITION: .... TECHNIQUE: ....

KEY DETAILS: ....

_____

_____

_____

_____

_____

_____

POSITION: .... TECHNIQUE: ....

KEY DETAILS: ....

_____

_____

_____

_____

_____

_____

TRAINING PARTNER: NOTES: GOAL: ....

_____   _____

_____   _____

_____   _____

_____   _____

_____   _____

_____   _____

ONE IMPORTANT THING I WANT TO REMEMBER ABOUT TODAY:

_____

_____

_____

DATE: _____ INSTRUCTOR: _____

BELT RANK: _____ WEIGHT: _____ ☐ GI ☐ NOGI ☐ BOTH

POSITION: _____ TECHNIQUE: _____

KEY DETAILS: _____

_____

_____

_____

_____

_____

_____

POSITION: _____ TECHNIQUE: _____

KEY DETAILS: _____

_____

_____

_____

_____

_____

_____

POSITION: _____ TECHNIQUE: _____

KEY DETAILS: _____

_____

_____

_____

_____

_____

_____

POSITION: _____ TECHNIQUE: _____
KEY DETAILS: _____
_____
_____
_____
_____
_____
_____

POSITION: _____ TECHNIQUE: _____
KEY DETAILS: _____
_____
_____
_____
_____
_____
_____

TRAINING PARTNER:	NOTES:	GOAL:

ONE IMPORTANT THING I WANT TO REMEMBER ABOUT TODAY:
_____
_____
_____

DATE: _____ INSTRUCTOR: _____

BELT RANK: _____ WEIGHT: _____ ☐ GI ☐ NOGI ☐ BOTH

POSITION: _____ TECHNIQUE: _____
KEY DETAILS: _____
_____
_____
_____
_____
_____
_____

POSITION: _____ TECHNIQUE: _____
KEY DETAILS: _____
_____
_____
_____
_____
_____
_____

POSITION: _____ TECHNIQUE: _____
KEY DETAILS: _____
_____
_____
_____
_____
_____
_____

POSITION: .... TECHNIQUE: ....

KEY DETAILS: ....

_____

_____

_____

_____

_____

_____

_____

POSITION: .... TECHNIQUE: ....

KEY DETAILS: ....

_____

_____

_____

_____

_____

TRAINING PARTNER: NOTES: GOAL: ....

_____ _____

_____ _____

_____ _____

_____ _____

_____ _____

ONE IMPORTANT THING I WANT TO REMEMBER ABOUT TODAY:

_____

_____

_____

DATE: _____ INSTRUCTOR: _____

BELT RANK: _____ WEIGHT: _____ ☐ GI ☐ NOGI ☐ BOTH

POSITION: _____ TECHNIQUE: _____

KEY DETAILS: _____

_____

_____

_____

_____

_____

_____

POSITION: _____ TECHNIQUE: _____

KEY DETAILS: _____

_____

_____

_____

_____

_____

_____

POSITION: _____ TECHNIQUE: _____

KEY DETAILS: _____

_____

_____

_____

_____

_____

_____

POSITION: .... TECHNIQUE: ....
KEY DETAILS: ....

_____

_____

_____

_____

_____

_____

_____

_____

POSITION: .... TECHNIQUE: ....
KEY DETAILS: ....

_____

_____

_____

_____

_____

_____

TRAINING PARTNER:	NOTES:	GOAL:

ONE IMPORTANT THING I WANT TO REMEMBER ABOUT TODAY:

_____

_____

_____

DATE: _____ INSTRUCTOR: _____

BELT RANK: _____ WEIGHT: _____ ☐ GI ☐ NOGI ☐ BOTH

POSITION: _____ TECHNIQUE: _____
KEY DETAILS: _____

_____

_____

_____

_____

_____

_____

POSITION: _____ TECHNIQUE: _____
KEY DETAILS: _____

_____

_____

_____

_____

_____

_____

POSITION: _____ TECHNIQUE: _____
KEY DETAILS: _____

_____

_____

_____

_____

_____

_____

POSITION: .... TECHNIQUE: ....

KEY DETAILS: ....

....

....

....

....

....

....

POSITION: .... TECHNIQUE: ....

KEY DETAILS: ....

....

....

....

....

....

....

TRAINING PARTNER:	NOTES:	GOAL:

ONE IMPORTANT THING I WANT TO REMEMBER ABOUT TODAY:

....

....

....

DATE: _____ INSTRUCTOR: _____

BELT RANK: _____ WEIGHT: _____ ☐ GI ☐ NOGI ☐ BOTH

POSITION: _____ TECHNIQUE: _____

KEY DETAILS: _____

_____

_____

_____

_____

_____

_____

POSITION: _____ TECHNIQUE: _____

KEY DETAILS: _____

_____

_____

_____

_____

_____

_____

POSITION: _____ TECHNIQUE: _____

KEY DETAILS: _____

_____

_____

_____

_____

_____

_____

POSITION: _____ TECHNIQUE: _____

KEY DETAILS: _____

_____

_____

_____

_____

_____

_____

POSITION: _____ TECHNIQUE: _____

KEY DETAILS: _____

_____

_____

_____

_____

_____

TRAINING PARTNER: NOTES: GOAL: _____

ONE IMPORTANT THING I WANT TO REMEMBER ABOUT TODAY:

DATE: .... INSTRUCTOR: ....

BELT RANK: .... WEIGHT: .... ☐ GI ☐ NOGI ☐ BOTH

POSITION: .... TECHNIQUE: ....

KEY DETAILS: ....

_____

_____

_____

_____

_____

_____

_____

POSITION: .... TECHNIQUE: ....

KEY DETAILS: ....

_____

_____

_____

_____

_____

_____

_____

POSITION: .... TECHNIQUE: ....

KEY DETAILS: ....

_____

_____

_____

_____

_____

_____

_____

POSITION: _____ TECHNIQUE: _____

KEY DETAILS: _____
_____
_____
_____
_____
_____
_____
_____

POSITION: _____ TECHNIQUE: _____

KEY DETAILS: _____
_____
_____
_____
_____
_____
_____
_____

TRAINING PARTNER: NOTES: GOAL: _____

_____   _____
_____   _____
_____   _____
_____   _____
_____   _____
_____   _____

ONE IMPORTANT THING I WANT TO REMEMBER ABOUT TODAY:

_____
_____
_____

DATE: .... INSTRUCTOR: ....

BELT RANK: .... WEIGHT: .... ☐ GI ☐ NOGI ☐ BOTH

POSITION: .... TECHNIQUE: ....

KEY DETAILS: ....

....

....

....

....

....

....

....

POSITION: .... TECHNIQUE: ....

KEY DETAILS: ....

....

....

....

....

....

....

....

POSITION: .... TECHNIQUE: ....

KEY DETAILS: ....

....

....

....

....

....

....

POSITION: _____ TECHNIQUE: _____

KEY DETAILS: _____

_____

_____

_____

_____

_____

_____

_____

POSITION: _____ TECHNIQUE: _____

KEY DETAILS: _____

_____

_____

_____

_____

_____

_____

TRAINING PARTNER: NOTES: GOAL: _____

_____   _____

_____   _____

_____   _____

_____   _____

_____   _____

ONE IMPORTANT THING I WANT TO REMEMBER ABOUT TODAY:

_____

_____

_____

DATE: _____ INSTRUCTOR: _____
BELT RANK: _____ WEIGHT: _____ ☐ GI ☐ NOGI ☐ BOTH

POSITION: _____ TECHNIQUE: _____
KEY DETAILS: _____
_____
_____
_____
_____
_____
_____

POSITION: _____ TECHNIQUE: _____
KEY DETAILS: _____
_____
_____
_____
_____
_____
_____

POSITION: _____ TECHNIQUE: _____
KEY DETAILS: _____
_____
_____
_____
_____
_____
_____

POSITION: _____ TECHNIQUE: _____
KEY DETAILS: _____

_____

_____

_____

_____

_____

_____

_____

POSITION: _____ TECHNIQUE: _____
KEY DETAILS: _____

_____

_____

_____

_____

_____

_____

TRAINING PARTNER: NOTES: GOAL: _____

_____   _____

_____   _____

_____   _____

_____   _____

_____   _____

ONE IMPORTANT THING I WANT TO REMEMBER ABOUT TODAY:

_____

_____

_____

DATE: .... INSTRUCTOR: ....

BELT RANK: .... WEIGHT: .... ☐ GI ☐ NOGI ☐ BOTH

POSITION: .... TECHNIQUE: ....

KEY DETAILS: ....

_____

_____

_____

_____

_____

_____

POSITION: .... TECHNIQUE: ....

KEY DETAILS: ....

_____

_____

_____

_____

_____

_____

POSITION: .... TECHNIQUE: ....

KEY DETAILS: ....

_____

_____

_____

_____

_____

_____

POSITION: _____ TECHNIQUE: _____

KEY DETAILS: _____

_____

_____

_____

_____

_____

_____

_____

POSITION: _____ TECHNIQUE: _____

KEY DETAILS: _____

_____

_____

_____

_____

_____

TRAINING PARTNER: NOTES: GOAL: _____

_____	_____
_____	_____
_____	_____
_____	_____
_____	_____

ONE IMPORTANT THING I WANT TO REMEMBER ABOUT TODAY:

_____

_____

_____

DATE: _____ INSTRUCTOR: _____

BELT RANK: _____ WEIGHT: _____ ☐ GI ☐ NOGI ☐ BOTH

POSITION: _____ TECHNIQUE: _____

KEY DETAILS: _____

_____

_____

_____

_____

_____

_____

POSITION: _____ TECHNIQUE: _____

KEY DETAILS: _____

_____

_____

_____

_____

_____

_____

POSITION: _____ TECHNIQUE: _____

KEY DETAILS: _____

_____

_____

_____

_____

_____

_____

POSITION: _____ TECHNIQUE: _____

KEY DETAILS: _____

_____

_____

_____

_____

_____

_____

POSITION: _____ TECHNIQUE: _____

KEY DETAILS: _____

_____

_____

_____

_____

_____

_____

TRAINING PARTNER: NOTES: GOAL: _____

_____   _____

_____   _____

_____   _____

_____   _____

_____   _____

ONE IMPORTANT THING I WANT TO REMEMBER ABOUT TODAY:

_____

_____

_____

DATE: _____ INSTRUCTOR: _____

BELT RANK: _____ WEIGHT: _____ ☐ GI ☐ NOGI ☐ BOTH

POSITION: _____ TECHNIQUE: _____

KEY DETAILS: _____

_____

_____

_____

_____

_____

_____

POSITION: _____ TECHNIQUE: _____

KEY DETAILS: _____

_____

_____

_____

_____

_____

_____

POSITION: _____ TECHNIQUE: _____

KEY DETAILS: _____

_____

_____

_____

_____

_____

_____

POSITION: _____ TECHNIQUE: _____
KEY DETAILS: _____

_____
_____
_____
_____
_____
_____

POSITION: _____ TECHNIQUE: _____
KEY DETAILS: _____

_____
_____
_____
_____
_____

TRAINING PARTNER: NOTES: GOAL: _____

_____   _____
_____   _____
_____   _____
_____   _____
_____   _____

ONE IMPORTANT THING I WANT TO REMEMBER ABOUT TODAY:

_____
_____
_____

DATE: .... INSTRUCTOR: ....

BELT RANK: .... WEIGHT: .... ☐ GI ☐ NOGI ☐ BOTH

POSITION: .... TECHNIQUE: ....

KEY DETAILS: ....

....

....

....

....

....

....

....

POSITION: .... TECHNIQUE: ....

KEY DETAILS: ....

....

....

....

....

....

....

....

POSITION: .... TECHNIQUE: ....

KEY DETAILS: ....

....

....

....

....

....

....

....

POSITION: .... TECHNIQUE: ....

KEY DETAILS: ....

_____

_____

_____

_____

_____

_____

_____

POSITION: .... TECHNIQUE: ....

KEY DETAILS: ....

_____

_____

_____

_____

_____

_____

_____

TRAINING PARTNER: NOTES: GOAL: ....

ONE IMPORTANT THING I WANT TO REMEMBER ABOUT TODAY:

_____

_____

_____

DATE: _____ INSTRUCTOR: _____

BELT RANK: _____ WEIGHT: _____ ☐ GI ☐ NOGI ☐ BOTH

POSITION: _____ TECHNIQUE: _____

KEY DETAILS: _____

_____

_____

_____

_____

_____

_____

_____

POSITION: _____ TECHNIQUE: _____

KEY DETAILS: _____

_____

_____

_____

_____

_____

_____

_____

POSITION: _____ TECHNIQUE: _____

KEY DETAILS: _____

_____

_____

_____

_____

_____

_____

_____

POSITION: _____ TECHNIQUE: _____

KEY DETAILS: _____

_____

_____

_____

_____

_____

_____

_____

POSITION: _____ TECHNIQUE: _____

KEY DETAILS: _____

_____

_____

_____

_____

_____

_____

_____

TRAINING PARTNER:	NOTES:	GOAL:

ONE IMPORTANT THING I WANT TO REMEMBER ABOUT TODAY:

_____

_____

_____

DATE: .... INSTRUCTOR: ....

BELT RANK: .... WEIGHT: .... ☐ GI ☐ NOGI ☐ BOTH

POSITION: .... TECHNIQUE: ....

KEY DETAILS: ....

_____

_____

_____

_____

_____

_____

POSITION: .... TECHNIQUE: ....

KEY DETAILS: ....

_____

_____

_____

_____

_____

_____

POSITION: .... TECHNIQUE: ....

KEY DETAILS: ....

_____

_____

_____

_____

_____

_____

POSITION: _____ TECHNIQUE: _____

KEY DETAILS: _____

_____

_____

_____

_____

_____

_____

_____

POSITION: _____ TECHNIQUE: _____

KEY DETAILS: _____

_____

_____

_____

_____

_____

_____

TRAINING PARTNER:	NOTES:	GOAL:

ONE IMPORTANT THING I WANT TO REMEMBER ABOUT TODAY:

_____

_____

_____

DATE: _____ INSTRUCTOR: _____

BELT RANK: _____ WEIGHT: _____ ☐ GI ☐ NOGI ☐ BOTH

POSITION: _____ TECHNIQUE: _____

KEY DETAILS: _____

_____

_____

_____

_____

_____

_____

POSITION: _____ TECHNIQUE: _____

KEY DETAILS: _____

_____

_____

_____

_____

_____

_____

POSITION: _____ TECHNIQUE: _____

KEY DETAILS: _____

_____

_____

_____

_____

_____

_____

POSITION: _____ TECHNIQUE: _____
KEY DETAILS: _____

_____
_____
_____
_____
_____
_____
_____

POSITION: _____ TECHNIQUE: _____
KEY DETAILS: _____

_____
_____
_____
_____
_____
_____
_____

TRAINING PARTNER: NOTES: GOAL: _____

_____   _____
_____   _____
_____   _____
_____   _____
_____   _____

ONE IMPORTANT THING I WANT TO REMEMBER ABOUT TODAY:

_____
_____
_____

DATE: _____ INSTRUCTOR: _____

BELT RANK: _____ WEIGHT: _____ ☐ GI ☐ NOGI ☐ BOTH

POSITION: _____ TECHNIQUE: _____

KEY DETAILS: _____

_____

_____

_____

_____

_____

_____

POSITION: _____ TECHNIQUE: _____

KEY DETAILS: _____

_____

_____

_____

_____

_____

_____

POSITION: _____ TECHNIQUE: _____

KEY DETAILS: _____

_____

_____

_____

_____

_____

_____

POSITION: _____ TECHNIQUE: _____

KEY DETAILS: _____

_____

_____

_____

_____

_____

_____

POSITION: _____ TECHNIQUE: _____

KEY DETAILS: _____

_____

_____

_____

_____

_____

_____

TRAINING PARTNER: NOTES: GOAL: _____

ONE IMPORTANT THING I WANT TO REMEMBER ABOUT TODAY:

_____

_____

_____

DATE: _____ INSTRUCTOR: _____

BELT RANK: _____ WEIGHT: _____ ☐ GI ☐ NOGI ☐ BOTH

POSITION: _____ TECHNIQUE: _____

KEY DETAILS: _____

_____

_____

_____

_____

_____

_____

_____

POSITION: _____ TECHNIQUE: _____

KEY DETAILS: _____

_____

_____

_____

_____

_____

_____

_____

POSITION: _____ TECHNIQUE: _____

KEY DETAILS: _____

_____

_____

_____

_____

_____

_____

_____

POSITION: .... TECHNIQUE: ....

KEY DETAILS: ....

_____

_____

_____

_____

_____

_____

_____

POSITION: .... TECHNIQUE: ....

KEY DETAILS: ....

_____

_____

_____

_____

_____

_____

TRAINING PARTNER: NOTES: GOAL: ....

_____   _____   _____

_____   _____   _____

_____   _____   _____

_____   _____   _____

_____   _____   _____

ONE IMPORTANT THING I WANT TO REMEMBER ABOUT TODAY:

_____

_____

_____

DATE: _____ INSTRUCTOR: _____

BELT RANK: _____ WEIGHT: _____ ☐ GI ☐ NOGI ☐ BOTH

POSITION: _____ TECHNIQUE: _____

KEY DETAILS: _____

_____

_____

_____

_____

_____

_____

POSITION: _____ TECHNIQUE: _____

KEY DETAILS: _____

_____

_____

_____

_____

_____

_____

POSITION: _____ TECHNIQUE: _____

KEY DETAILS: _____

_____

_____

_____

_____

_____

_____

POSITION: .... TECHNIQUE: ....

KEY DETAILS: ....

_____

_____

_____

_____

_____

_____

POSITION: .... TECHNIQUE: ....

KEY DETAILS: ....

_____

_____

_____

_____

_____

_____

TRAINING PARTNER: NOTES: GOAL: ....

_____   _____

_____   _____

_____   _____

_____   _____

_____   _____

ONE IMPORTANT THING I WANT TO REMEMBER ABOUT TODAY:

_____

_____

_____

DATE: .... INSTRUCTOR: ....

BELT RANK: .... WEIGHT: .... ☐ GI ☐ NOGI ☐ BOTH

POSITION: .... TECHNIQUE: ....

KEY DETAILS: ....

POSITION: .... TECHNIQUE: ....

KEY DETAILS: ....

POSITION: .... TECHNIQUE: ....

KEY DETAILS: ....

POSITION: _____ **TECHNIQUE:** _____

KEY DETAILS: _____

_____

_____

_____

_____

_____

_____

POSITION: _____ **TECHNIQUE:** _____

KEY DETAILS: _____

_____

_____

_____

_____

_____

TRAINING PARTNER:	NOTES:	GOAL:

ONE IMPORTANT THING I WANT TO REMEMBER ABOUT TODAY:

_____

_____

_____

DATE: _____ INSTRUCTOR: _____

BELT RANK: _____ WEIGHT: _____ ☐ GI ☐ NOGI ☐ BOTH

POSITION: _____ TECHNIQUE: _____

KEY DETAILS: _____

_____

_____

_____

_____

_____

_____

_____

POSITION: _____ TECHNIQUE: _____

KEY DETAILS: _____

_____

_____

_____

_____

_____

_____

POSITION: _____ TECHNIQUE: _____

KEY DETAILS: _____

_____

_____

_____

_____

_____

_____

POSITION: .... TECHNIQUE: ....
KEY DETAILS: ....

_____

_____

_____

_____

_____

_____

_____

_____

POSITION: .... TECHNIQUE: ....
KEY DETAILS: ....

_____

_____

_____

_____

_____

_____

_____

TRAINING PARTNER: NOTES: GOAL: ....

ONE IMPORTANT THING I WANT TO REMEMBER ABOUT TODAY:

DATE: .... INSTRUCTOR: ....

BELT RANK: .... WEIGHT: .... ☐ GI ☐ NOGI ☐ BOTH

POSITION: .... TECHNIQUE: ....

KEY DETAILS: ....

_____

_____

_____

_____

_____

_____

_____

POSITION: .... TECHNIQUE: ....

KEY DETAILS: ....

_____

_____

_____

_____

_____

_____

_____

POSITION: .... TECHNIQUE: ....

KEY DETAILS: ....

_____

_____

_____

_____

_____

_____

_____

POSITION: _____ TECHNIQUE: _____

KEY DETAILS: _____

_____

_____

_____

_____

_____

_____

POSITION: _____ TECHNIQUE: _____

KEY DETAILS: _____

_____

_____

_____

_____

_____

TRAINING PARTNER: NOTES: GOAL: _____

TRAINING PARTNER	NOTES	GOAL

ONE IMPORTANT THING I WANT TO REMEMBER ABOUT TODAY:

_____

_____

_____

DATE: _____ INSTRUCTOR: _____

BELT RANK: _____ WEIGHT: _____ ☐ GI ☐ NOGI ☐ BOTH

POSITION: _____ TECHNIQUE: _____

KEY DETAILS: _____

_____

_____

_____

_____

_____

_____

POSITION: _____ TECHNIQUE: _____

KEY DETAILS: _____

_____

_____

_____

_____

_____

_____

POSITION: _____ TECHNIQUE: _____

KEY DETAILS: _____

_____

_____

_____

_____

_____

_____

POSITION: _____ TECHNIQUE: _____

KEY DETAILS: _____

_____

_____

_____

_____

_____

_____

_____

POSITION: _____ TECHNIQUE: _____

KEY DETAILS: _____

_____

_____

_____

_____

_____

TRAINING PARTNER: NOTES: GOAL: _____

_____   _____

_____   _____

_____   _____

_____   _____

ONE IMPORTANT THING I WANT TO REMEMBER ABOUT TODAY:

_____

_____

_____

DATE: _____ INSTRUCTOR: _____

BELT RANK: _____ WEIGHT: _____ ☐ GI ☐ NOGI ☐ BOTH

POSITION: _____ TECHNIQUE: _____

KEY DETAILS: _____

_____

_____

_____

_____

_____

_____

POSITION: _____ TECHNIQUE: _____

KEY DETAILS: _____

_____

_____

_____

_____

_____

_____

POSITION: _____ TECHNIQUE: _____

KEY DETAILS: _____

_____

_____

_____

_____

_____

_____

SITION: .... **TECHNIQUE:** ....

Y DETAILS: ....

_____

_____

_____

_____

_____

_____

_____

SITION: .... **TECHNIQUE:** ....

Y DETAILS: ....

_____

_____

_____

_____

_____

_____

AINING PARTNER: **NOTES:**   **GOAL:** ....

_____   _____

_____   _____

_____   _____

_____   _____

_____   _____

ONE IMPORTANT THING I WANT TO REMEMBER ABOUT TODAY:

_____

_____

_____

DATE: _____ INSTRUCTOR: _____

BELT RANK: _____ WEIGHT: _____ ☐ GI ☐ NOGI ☐ BOTH

POSITION: _____ TECHNIQUE: _____

KEY DETAILS: _____

_____

_____

_____

_____

_____

_____

POSITION: _____ TECHNIQUE: _____

KEY DETAILS: _____

_____

_____

_____

_____

_____

_____

POSITION: _____ TECHNIQUE: _____

KEY DETAILS: _____

_____

_____

_____

_____

_____

_____

POSITION: _____ TECHNIQUE: _____

KEY DETAILS: _____

_____

_____

_____

_____

_____

POSITION: _____ TECHNIQUE: _____

KEY DETAILS: _____

_____

_____

_____

_____

_____

TRAINING PARTNER: NOTES: GOAL: _____

ONE IMPORTANT THING I WANT TO REMEMBER ABOUT TODAY:

DATE: _____ INSTRUCTOR: _____

BELT RANK: _____ WEIGHT: _____ ☐ GI ☐ NOGI ☐ BOTH

POSITION: _____ TECHNIQUE: _____

KEY DETAILS: _____

_____

_____

_____

_____

_____

_____

POSITION: _____ TECHNIQUE: _____

KEY DETAILS: _____

_____

_____

_____

_____

_____

_____

POSITION: _____ TECHNIQUE: _____

KEY DETAILS: _____

_____

_____

_____

_____

_____

_____

POSITION: .... TECHNIQUE: ....

KEY DETAILS: ....
_____
_____
_____
_____
_____
_____

POSITION: .... TECHNIQUE: ....

KEY DETAILS: ....
_____
_____
_____
_____
_____
_____

TRAINING PARTNER: NOTES: GOAL: ....

ONE IMPORTANT THING I WANT TO REMEMBER ABOUT TODAY:

_____
_____
_____

DATE: _____ INSTRUCTOR: _____

BELT RANK: _____ WEIGHT: _____ ☐ GI ☐ NOGI ☐ BOTH

POSITION: _____ TECHNIQUE: _____

KEY DETAILS: _____

_____

_____

_____

_____

_____

POSITION: _____ TECHNIQUE: _____

KEY DETAILS: _____

_____

_____

_____

_____

_____

POSITION: _____ TECHNIQUE: _____

KEY DETAILS: _____

_____

_____

_____

_____

_____

POSITION: .... TECHNIQUE: ....

KEY DETAILS: ....

_____

_____

_____

_____

_____

_____

_____

POSITION: .... TECHNIQUE: ....

KEY DETAILS: ....

_____

_____

_____

_____

_____

_____

_____

TRAINING PARTNER: NOTES: GOAL: ....

ONE IMPORTANT THING I WANT TO REMEMBER ABOUT TODAY:

DATE: .... INSTRUCTOR: ....

BELT RANK: .... WEIGHT: .... ☐ GI ☐ NOGI ☐ BOTH

POSITION: .... TECHNIQUE: ....

KEY DETAILS: ....

_____

_____

_____

_____

_____

_____

POSITION: .... TECHNIQUE: ....

KEY DETAILS: ....

_____

_____

_____

_____

_____

_____

POSITION: .... TECHNIQUE: ....

KEY DETAILS: ....

_____

_____

_____

_____

_____

_____

POSITION: _____ TECHNIQUE: _____
KEY DETAILS: _____

_____

_____

_____

_____

_____

_____

POSITION: _____ TECHNIQUE: _____
KEY DETAILS: _____

_____

_____

_____

_____

_____

TRAINING PARTNER: NOTES: GOAL: _____

_____   _____

_____   _____

_____   _____

_____   _____

ONE IMPORTANT THING I WANT TO REMEMBER ABOUT TODAY:

_____

_____

_____

DATE: _____ INSTRUCTOR: _____

BELT RANK: _____ WEIGHT: _____ ☐ GI ☐ NOGI ☐ BOTH

POSITION: _____ TECHNIQUE: _____

KEY DETAILS: _____

_____

_____

_____

_____

_____

_____

_____

POSITION: _____ TECHNIQUE: _____

KEY DETAILS: _____

_____

_____

_____

_____

_____

_____

_____

POSITION: _____ TECHNIQUE: _____

KEY DETAILS: _____

_____

_____

_____

_____

_____

_____

_____

POSITION: .... **TECHNIQUE:** ....

KEY DETAILS: _____

_____

_____

_____

_____

_____

_____

_____

POSITION: .... **TECHNIQUE:** ....

KEY DETAILS: _____

_____

_____

_____

_____

_____

_____

_____

TRAINING PARTNER: **NOTES:**   **GOAL:** ....

_____   _____

_____   _____

_____   _____

_____   _____

_____   _____

ONE IMPORTANT THING I WANT TO REMEMBER ABOUT TODAY:

_____

_____

_____

DATE: .... INSTRUCTOR: ....

BELT RANK: .... WEIGHT: .... ☐ GI ☐ NOGI ☐ BOTH

POSITION: .... TECHNIQUE: ....

KEY DETAILS: ....

_____

_____

_____

_____

_____

_____

POSITION: .... TECHNIQUE: ....

KEY DETAILS: ....

_____

_____

_____

_____

_____

_____

POSITION: .... TECHNIQUE: ....

KEY DETAILS: ....

_____

_____

_____

_____

_____

_____

POSITION: .... **TECHNIQUE:** ....

KEY DETAILS: _____

_____

_____

_____

_____

_____

_____

_____

POSITION: .... **TECHNIQUE:** ....

KEY DETAILS: _____

_____

_____

_____

_____

_____

_____

TRAINING PARTNER: **NOTES:**   **GOAL:** ....

ONE IMPORTANT THING I WANT TO REMEMBER ABOUT TODAY:

DATE: _____ INSTRUCTOR: _____

BELT RANK: _____ WEIGHT: _____ ☐ GI ☐ NOGI ☐ BOTH

POSITION: _____ TECHNIQUE: _____

KEY DETAILS: _____

_____

_____

_____

_____

_____

_____

POSITION: _____ TECHNIQUE: _____

KEY DETAILS: _____

_____

_____

_____

_____

_____

_____

POSITION: _____ TECHNIQUE: _____

KEY DETAILS: _____

_____

_____

_____

_____

_____

_____

POSITION: .... **TECHNIQUE:** ....

KEY DETAILS: ....

....

....

....

....

....

....

POSITION: .... **TECHNIQUE:** ....

KEY DETAILS: ....

....

....

....

....

....

TRAINING PARTNER: **NOTES:**   **GOAL:** ....

TRAINING PARTNER	NOTES / GOAL
....	....
....	....
....	....
....	....
....	....

ONE IMPORTANT THING I WANT TO REMEMBER ABOUT TODAY:

....

....

....

DATE: _____   INSTRUCTOR: _____

BELT RANK: _____   WEIGHT: _____   ☐ GI   ☐ NOGI   ☐ BOTH

POSITION: _____   TECHNIQUE: _____

KEY DETAILS: _____

_____

_____

_____

_____

_____

_____

POSITION: _____   TECHNIQUE: _____

KEY DETAILS: _____

_____

_____

_____

_____

_____

_____

POSITION: _____   TECHNIQUE: _____

KEY DETAILS: _____

_____

_____

_____

_____

_____

_____

POSITION: .... TECHNIQUE: ....

KEY DETAILS: ....

_____

_____

_____

_____

_____

_____

_____

POSITION: .... TECHNIQUE: ....

KEY DETAILS: ....

_____

_____

_____

_____

_____

_____

TRAINING PARTNER: NOTES: GOAL: ....

TRAINING PARTNER	NOTES
_____	_____
_____	_____
_____	_____
_____	_____
_____	_____

ONE IMPORTANT THING I WANT TO REMEMBER ABOUT TODAY:

_____

_____

_____

DATE: _____ INSTRUCTOR: _____

BELT RANK: _____ WEIGHT: _____ ☐ GI ☐ NOGI ☐ BOTH

POSITION: _____ TECHNIQUE: _____

KEY DETAILS: _____

_____

_____

_____

_____

_____

_____

_____

POSITION: _____ TECHNIQUE: _____

KEY DETAILS: _____

_____

_____

_____

_____

_____

_____

_____

POSITION: _____ TECHNIQUE: _____

KEY DETAILS: _____

_____

_____

_____

_____

_____

_____

_____

POSITION: .... **TECHNIQUE:** ....

KEY DETAILS: ....

_____

_____

_____

_____

_____

_____

POSITION: .... **TECHNIQUE:** ....

KEY DETAILS: ....

_____

_____

_____

_____

_____

_____

TRAINING PARTNER: **NOTES:**   **GOAL:** ....

_____   _____

_____   _____

_____   _____

_____   _____

_____   _____

ONE IMPORTANT THING I WANT TO REMEMBER ABOUT TODAY:

....

_____

_____

DATE: _____ INSTRUCTOR: _____

BELT RANK: _____ WEIGHT: _____ ☐ GI ☐ NOGI ☐ BOTH

POSITION: _____ TECHNIQUE: _____

KEY DETAILS: _____

_____

_____

_____

_____

_____

_____

_____

POSITION: _____ TECHNIQUE: _____

KEY DETAILS: _____

_____

_____

_____

_____

_____

_____

_____

POSITION: _____ TECHNIQUE: _____

KEY DETAILS: _____

_____

_____

_____

_____

_____

_____

_____

POSITION: _____ TECHNIQUE: _____

KEY DETAILS: _____

_____

_____

_____

_____

_____

_____

POSITION: _____ TECHNIQUE: _____

KEY DETAILS: _____

_____

_____

_____

_____

_____

_____

TRAINING PARTNER: NOTES: GOAL: _____

_____   _____

_____   _____

_____   _____

_____   _____

_____   _____

ONE IMPORTANT THING I WANT TO REMEMBER ABOUT TODAY:

_____

_____

_____

DATE: _____ INSTRUCTOR: _____

BELT RANK: _____ WEIGHT: _____ ☐ GI ☐ NOGI ☐ BOTH

POSITION: _____ TECHNIQUE: _____

KEY DETAILS: _____

_____

_____

_____

_____

_____

_____

_____

POSITION: _____ TECHNIQUE: _____

KEY DETAILS: _____

_____

_____

_____

_____

_____

_____

_____

POSITION: _____ TECHNIQUE: _____

KEY DETAILS: _____

_____

_____

_____

_____

_____

_____

_____

POSITION: _____ TECHNIQUE: _____

KEY DETAILS: _____

_____

_____

_____

_____

_____

POSITION: _____ TECHNIQUE: _____

KEY DETAILS: _____

_____

_____

_____

_____

_____

TRAINING PARTNER: NOTES: GOAL: _____

_____	_____
_____	_____
_____	_____
_____	_____
_____	_____

ONE IMPORTANT THING I WANT TO REMEMBER ABOUT TODAY:

_____

_____

_____

DATE: .... INSTRUCTOR: ....

BELT RANK: .... WEIGHT: .... ☐ GI ☐ NOGI ☐ BOTH

POSITION: .... TECHNIQUE: ....

KEY DETAILS: ....

_____

_____

_____

_____

_____

_____

POSITION: .... TECHNIQUE: ....

KEY DETAILS: ....

_____

_____

_____

_____

_____

_____

POSITION: .... TECHNIQUE: ....

KEY DETAILS: ....

_____

_____

_____

_____

_____

_____

POSITION: _____ TECHNIQUE: _____
KEY DETAILS: _____

_____
_____
_____
_____
_____
_____
_____
_____
_____
_____

POSITION: _____ TECHNIQUE: _____
KEY DETAILS: _____

_____
_____
_____
_____
_____
_____
_____

TRAINING PARTNER: NOTES: GOAL: _____

_____   _____
_____   _____
_____   _____
_____   _____
_____   _____

ONE IMPORTANT THING I WANT TO REMEMBER ABOUT TODAY:

_____
_____
_____

DATE: _____ INSTRUCTOR: _____

BELT RANK: _____ WEIGHT: _____ ☐ GI ☐ NOGI ☐ BOTH

POSITION: _____ TECHNIQUE: _____

KEY DETAILS: _____

_____

_____

_____

_____

_____

_____

POSITION: _____ TECHNIQUE: _____

KEY DETAILS: _____

_____

_____

_____

_____

_____

_____

POSITION: _____ TECHNIQUE: _____

KEY DETAILS: _____

_____

_____

_____

_____

_____

_____

POSITION: _____ TECHNIQUE: _____
KEY DETAILS: _____

_____
_____
_____
_____
_____
_____

POSITION: _____ TECHNIQUE: _____
KEY DETAILS: _____

_____
_____
_____
_____
_____
_____

TRAINING PARTNER: NOTES: GOAL: _____

_____   _____
_____   _____
_____   _____
_____   _____
_____   _____

ONE IMPORTANT THING I WANT TO REMEMBER ABOUT TODAY:

_____
_____
_____

DATE: _____ INSTRUCTOR: _____

BELT RANK: _____ WEIGHT: _____ ☐ GI ☐ NOGI ☐ BOTH

POSITION: _____ TECHNIQUE: _____

KEY DETAILS: _____

_____

_____

_____

_____

_____

_____

POSITION: _____ TECHNIQUE: _____

KEY DETAILS: _____

_____

_____

_____

_____

_____

_____

POSITION: _____ TECHNIQUE: _____

KEY DETAILS: _____

_____

_____

_____

_____

_____

_____

SITION: _____ TECHNIQUE: _____

Y DETAILS: _____

_____

_____

_____

_____

_____

_____

SITION: _____ TECHNIQUE: _____

Y DETAILS: _____

_____

_____

_____

_____

_____

_____

AINING PARTNER: NOTES: GOAL: _____

_____   _____

_____   _____

_____   _____

_____   _____

_____   _____

ONE IMPORTANT THING I WANT TO REMEMBER ABOUT TODAY:

_____

_____

_____

DATE: .... INSTRUCTOR: ....

BELT RANK: .... WEIGHT: .... ☐ GI ☐ NOGI ☐ BOTH

POSITION: .... TECHNIQUE: ....

KEY DETAILS: ....

_____

_____

_____

_____

_____

_____

_____

POSITION: .... TECHNIQUE: ....

KEY DETAILS: ....

_____

_____

_____

_____

_____

_____

_____

POSITION: .... TECHNIQUE: ....

KEY DETAILS: ....

_____

_____

_____

_____

_____

_____

_____

POSITION: _____ TECHNIQUE: _____

KEY DETAILS: _____

_____

_____

_____

_____

_____

_____

_____

POSITION: _____ TECHNIQUE: _____

KEY DETAILS: _____

_____

_____

_____

_____

_____

_____

TRAINING PARTNER: NOTES: GOAL: _____

TRAINING PARTNER	NOTES	GOAL

ONE IMPORTANT THING I WANT TO REMEMBER ABOUT TODAY:

_____

_____

_____

DATE: _____ INSTRUCTOR: _____

BELT RANK: _____ WEIGHT: _____ ☐ GI ☐ NOGI ☐ BOTH

POSITION: _____ TECHNIQUE: _____

KEY DETAILS: _____

_____

_____

_____

_____

_____

_____

_____

POSITION: _____ TECHNIQUE: _____

KEY DETAILS: _____

_____

_____

_____

_____

_____

_____

_____

POSITION: _____ TECHNIQUE: _____

KEY DETAILS: _____

_____

_____

_____

_____

_____

_____

_____

POSITION: _____ TECHNIQUE: _____
KEY DETAILS: _____
_____
_____
_____
_____
_____
_____

POSITION: _____ TECHNIQUE: _____
KEY DETAILS: _____
_____
_____
_____
_____
_____
_____

TRAINING PARTNER: NOTES: GOAL: _____

ONE IMPORTANT THING I WANT TO REMEMBER ABOUT TODAY:

_____
_____
_____

DATE: _____ INSTRUCTOR: _____

BELT RANK: _____ WEIGHT: _____ ☐ GI ☐ NOGI ☐ BOTH

POSITION: _____ TECHNIQUE: _____

KEY DETAILS: _____

_____

_____

_____

_____

_____

_____

_____

POSITION: _____ TECHNIQUE: _____

KEY DETAILS: _____

_____

_____

_____

_____

_____

_____

_____

POSITION: _____ TECHNIQUE: _____

KEY DETAILS: _____

_____

_____

_____

_____

_____

_____

_____

SITION: .... **TECHNIQUE:** ....
Y DETAILS: ....

_____

_____

_____

_____

_____

_____

SITION: .... **TECHNIQUE:** ....
Y DETAILS: ....

_____

_____

_____

_____

_____

AINING PARTNER: **NOTES:** **GOAL:** ....

_____	_____
_____	_____
_____	_____
_____	_____
_____	_____

ONE IMPORTANT THING I WANT TO REMEMBER ABOUT TODAY:

....

_____

....

DATE: _____ INSTRUCTOR: _____

BELT RANK: _____ WEIGHT: _____ ☐ GI ☐ NOGI ☐ BOTH

POSITION: _____ TECHNIQUE: _____

KEY DETAILS: _____

_____

_____

_____

_____

_____

_____

_____

POSITION: _____ TECHNIQUE: _____

KEY DETAILS: _____

_____

_____

_____

_____

_____

_____

POSITION: _____ TECHNIQUE: _____

KEY DETAILS: _____

_____

_____

_____

_____

_____

_____

SITION: .... **TECHNIQUE:** ....

Y DETAILS: ....

....

....

....

....

....

....

....

....

SITION: .... **TECHNIQUE:** ....

Y DETAILS: ....

....

....

....

....

....

....

....

AINING PARTNER:	NOTES:	GOAL: ....
....		....
....		....
....		....
....		....
....		....

ONE IMPORTANT THING I WANT TO REMEMBER ABOUT TODAY:

....

....

....

**IF YOU WOULD LIKE TO ORDER MORE JOURNALS
PLEASE VISIT COMBAT ARTS PRESS AT AMAZON.COM**

Made in the USA
San Bernardino, CA
16 February 2020

64560933R00076